But the clever rat had a solution.
He suggested that he and the cat jump on the ox's back
and guide him. The ox and cat quickly agreed.

As soon as the race began, the ox and his two passengers took the
lead. But just before they reached the finish line, the rat pushed
the cat into the river (and out of the race),
then leapt from the ox's back to be the first ashore—and the
winner of first place in the Chinese zodiac.

Zoodiac contains a maze for each animal in the Chinese zodiac,
from the crafty rat to the slow-moving pig.
You can find out which animal you are—and read more
about your animal sign—at the back of
the book. Good luck!

The Rat

Rats have a talent for making themselves at home—and they like company. So find your way into the rat's den!

The rat was clever
and cunning enough
to win the first place
in Chinese astrology.
This is not surprising,
as rats work hard to
reach their goals.

The Ox
The honest, hard-working ox pursues goals with confidence and patience. Be persistent like an ox and find your way through the maze from left to right.

牛

The ox is also known to be quiet and trustworthy. The Chinese Valentine's Day honours an ox who played matchmaker to a cowherd and a heavenly fairy.

The Tiger
Tigers are born leaders:
brave, generous,
loyal and wise.
Find your way from the
Tiger Temple to the
waterhole—and prove
that you too can be a
leader!

虎

Even though tigers sometimes have difficulty making up their minds, the tiger is considered lucky by gamblers— but they forget that the tiger is also dangerous, and many gamblers lose everything.

The Rabbit
The trusting rabbit will always welcome a travelling salesman. Here the carrot seller is eager to find his own way to the rabbit's den.

Chinese legends say that if you look closely at the full moon, you can see the Jade Rabbit in the Moon Palace, singing together with the Moon Fairy.

The Dragon

Roll out the red carpet! Dragons expect it—and often deserve it. Help the dragon up the stairs to the Big Candle without leaving the red carpet.

龍

The dragon is the symbol of Chinese imperial power. Emperors were considered to be real dragons and the sons of the Heavenly God.

The Snake
Snakes are curious, organised and fun-loving—and clever enough to reach the tai-chi temple without stepping over any snakes. Are you?

蛇

Snakes are mysterious creatures that have always been feared as well as worshipped. Although some are deadly, they have also become symbols of medicine and healing.

The Horse

Horses are independent and like to travel. Travel by boat or road from the statue of the white horse on the left to the manger of hay on the right.

Horses are also known to be wise, talented and clever with money—the Roman Emperor Caligula thought his horse was so clever he made it a priest and senator!

The Sheep
Sensitive, artistic, gentle sheep don't like conflict—they prefer to relax. Find which of the eight gates leads to the deckchair.

The sheep features in many sayings. For example, "a wolf in sheep's clothing" is somebody who pretends to be friendly but has evil intentions.

The Monkey

Monkeys are original, independent and intelligent—and rarely listen to advice. With this maze, go in one ear and out the other!

猴

The legendary Monkey
King travelled on a cloud
and could transform
himself into 72 other
creatures. His story is
a favourite in
Chinese literature.

The Rooster

Roosters have a good eye for everything, be it fashion, art or character. So find your way to the rooster's eye from any of the maze's entrances.

Roosters are also brave, funny, sincere, generous and thoughtful—no wonder they are respected by farmers all over the world!

The Dog
Dogs are brave, but not stupid! Rather than swimming through crocodile-infested waters to get at the bone, they'd find another way. Can you?

犬

Faithful, responsible
and trustworthy,
dogs are often called
"Man's Best Friend".
Sadly, people do not
always deserve to be
called "Dog's Best
Friend"!

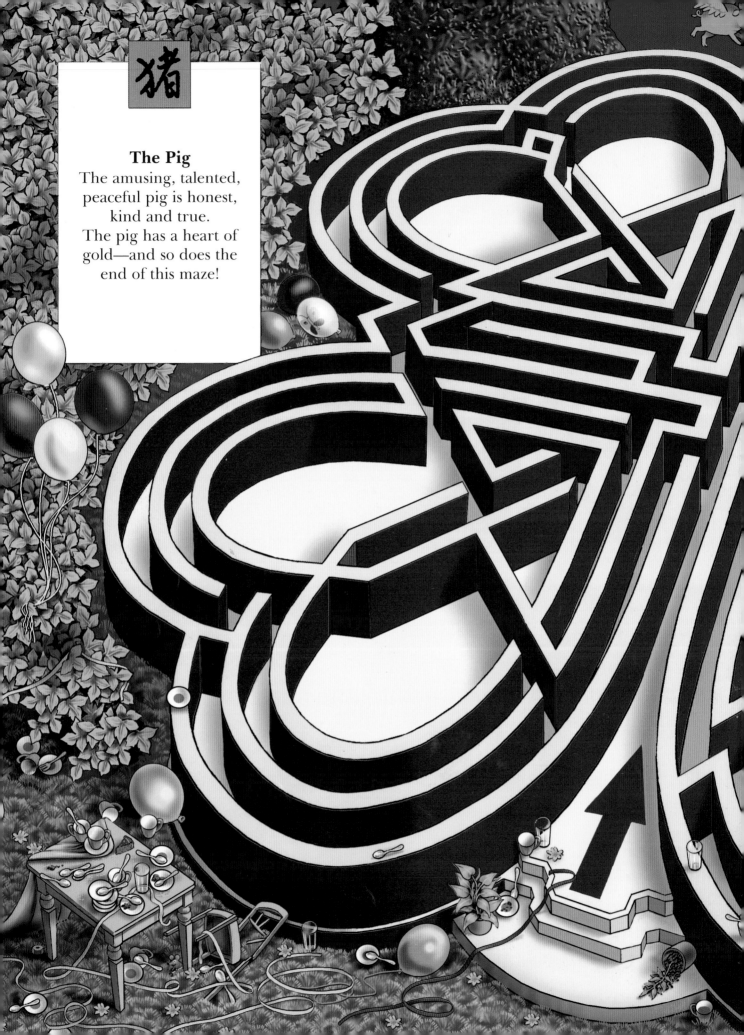

The Pig
The amusing, talented, peaceful pig is honest, kind and true. The pig has a heart of gold—and so does the end of this maze!

In Chinese literature, the Pig Man travelled with the Monkey King— and with his love of parties, he really livened up the story!

Going through a maze can bring out the worst in anyone! In addition to their positive qualities, the animals of the zodiac also have some less desirable traits …
See if you recognise yourself in these descriptions—but don't forget, there are exceptions!

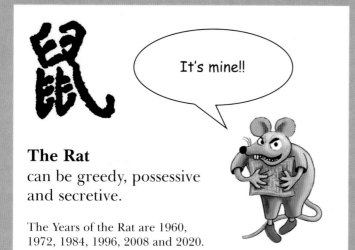

It's mine!!

The Rat
can be greedy, possessive and secretive.

The Years of the Rat are 1960, 1972, 1984, 1996, 2008 and 2020.

Boring…

The Ox
can be dull and gloomy.

The Years of the Ox are 1961, 1973, 1985, 1997, 2009 and 2021.

Who said I was cheating?

The Tiger
can be vain, quarrelsome and reckless.

The Years of the Tiger are 1950, 1962, 1974, 1986, 1998 and 2010.

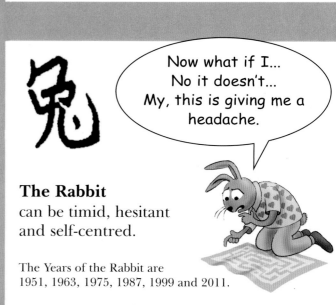

Now what if I… No it doesn't… My, this is giving me a headache.

The Rabbit
can be timid, hesitant and self-centred.

The Years of the Rabbit are 1951, 1963, 1975, 1987, 1999 and 2011.

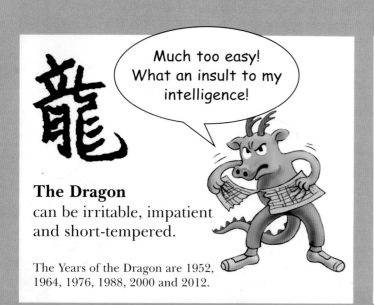

Much too easy! What an insult to my intelligence!

The Dragon
can be irritable, impatient and short-tempered.

The Years of the Dragon are 1952, 1964, 1976, 1988, 2000 and 2012.

I shall take the secret to my grave…

The Snake
can be cruel, pessimistic and jealous.

The Years of the Snake are 1953, 1965, 1977, 1989, 2001 and 2013.

When you check the year of your birth against the signs of the Chinese zodiac, remember that the Chinese calendar is based on the lunar cycle. So the Chinese New Year can occur in January or even February.

The Horse
can be careless, irresponsible and a show-off.

The Years of the Horse are 1954, 1966, 1978, 1990, 2002 and 2014.

The Sheep
can be lazy, vengeful and impractical.

The Years of the Sheep (sometimes called the Goat) are 1955, 1967, 1979, 1991, 2003 and 2015.

The Monkey
can be restless, unpredictable and over-optimistic.

The Years of the Monkey are 1956, 1968, 1980, 1992, 2004 and 2016.

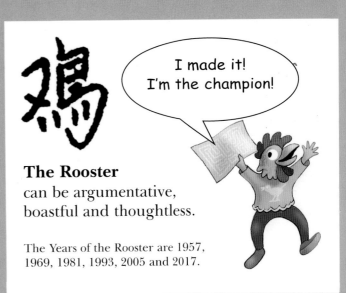

The Rooster
can be argumentative, boastful and thoughtless.

The Years of the Rooster are 1957, 1969, 1981, 1993, 2005 and 2017.

The Dog
can be nervous, suspicious and bad-tempered.

The Years of the Dog are 1958, 1970, 1982, 1994, 2006 and 2018.

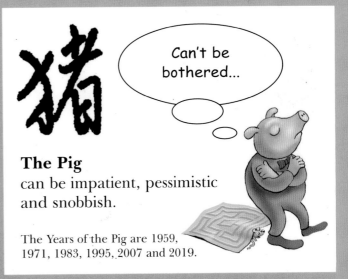

The Pig
can be impatient, pessimistic and snobbish.

The Years of the Pig are 1959, 1971, 1983, 1995, 2007 and 2019.

The Rat

The Ox

The Tiger

The Rabbit

The Dragon

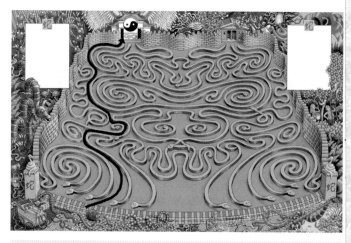

The Snake

The Horse

The Sheep

The Monkey

The Rooster

The Dog

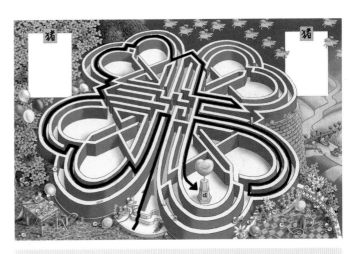

The Pig

Rolf Heimann, the creator of this book, is a dragon. That means he's a perfectionist who likes to make the rules. And because dragons are very demanding, he's added some difficult tasks for you.

The following things have been hidden in each maze:
A fish, a butterfly, a fork, a peace symbol , a nut  , a heart, a star, a mushroom, a key, a bird and a mouse.
And last, but not least, Rolf has hidden an outline of Australia. He's done that in all his pictures since he became an Australian citizen (and he never forgets Tasmania).

Published by Little Hare Books
45 Cooper Street, Surry Hills
NSW 2010 AUSTRALIA

National Library of Australia
Cataloguing-in-Publication entry

Heimann, Rolf, 1940-.
Zoodiac : the year of the maze.

For children.
ISBN 1 877003 04 2.

1. Maze puzzles - Juvenile literature. I. Title.

793.73

Designed by ANTART
Printed in Hong Kong

5 4 3 2 1